Crafts for Kids Who Are Wild About
Rainforests

Crafts for Kids Who Are

WILD
ABOUT
RAINFORESTS

By Kathy Ross
Illustrated by Sharon Lane Holm

The Millbrook Press   Brookfield, Connecticut

For my brother Rick, who is more fun than a forest full of monkeys!—K.R.
For my big sister Christine—S.L.H.

Library of Congress Cataloging-in-Publication Data
Ross, Kathy (Katharine Reynolds), 1948–
Crafts for kids who are wild about rainforests / by Kathy Ross ; illustrated by Sharon Lane Holm.
p. cm.
Summary: Introduces the world of rainforest plants and animals through twenty simple craft projects.
ISBN 0-7613-0117-8 (lib. bdg.)   ISBN 0-7613-0277-8 (pbk.)
1. Handicraft—Juvenile literature. 2. Rain forests in art—Juvenile literature.
3. Rain forest animals in art—Juvenile literature. [1. Handicraft. 2. Rain forests in art.
3. Rain forest animals in art.] I. Holm, Sharon Lane, ill. II. Title.
TT160.R714226 1997
745.5—dc20 96–35802 CIP AC

Published by The Millbrook Press, Inc.
2 Old New Milford Road
Brookfield, Connecticut 06804
//www.neca.com/mall/millbrook

Contents

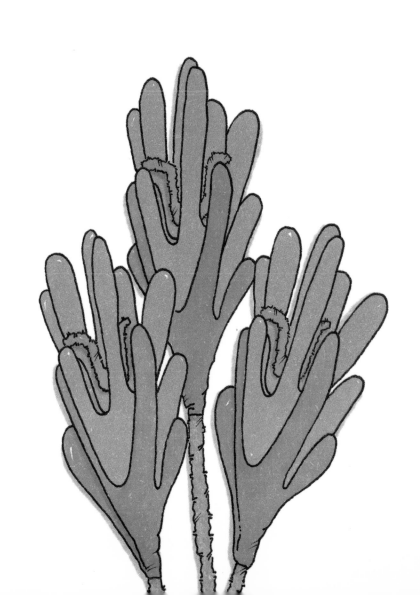

Introduction

Rainforests are the thick tangle of trees and plants that grow in the warm, wet lands near the equator. These forests make up less than one twentieth of the Earth's land, but scientists believe that the plants and animals found in the rainforests account for more than half of the species found on this planet.

More than 1,000 different groups of people live in tropical forests. Many medicines come from the trees and plants found only in our rainforests. The rainforests are also an important source of oxygen for our planet, and they affect weather and Earth's atmosphere, too.

Yet people's destruction of the rainforests continues—and we lose 50 million acres (20 million hectares) of this valuable land each year.

This book contains models of just a few of the amazing number of plants and animals that are part of the rainforests. You can add more details to your projects or give them more accurate coloring by looking for pictures and more information on the plants and animals you make. Learning more about rainforests is an important step in understanding the importance of saving them.

Kathy Ross

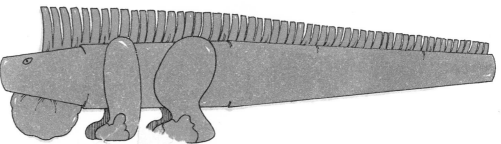

Rainforest Layers

Here is what you need:

large jar with lid
modeling clay
brown tissue paper
two or more shades of green tissue paper
sticks and twigs
Easter grass
white glue
masking tape
marker

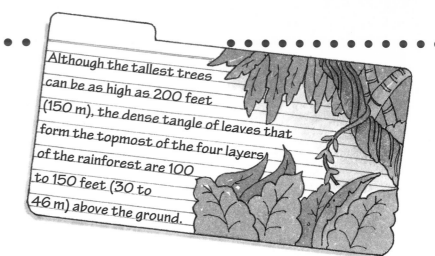

Although the tallest trees can be as high as 200 feet (150 m), the dense tangle of leaves that form the topmost of the four layers of the rainforest are 100 to 150 feet (30 to 46 m) above the ground.

Here is what you do:

Press a ball of clay onto the inside surface of the jar lid. Do not press it onto the sides of the lid, because you will not be able to put the lid back on the jar.

Break two sticks so that they are as long as the jar. Press them into the clay to make trees. Crumple some green or brown tissue paper and glue it around the top of the sticks to make the leaves. These tall trees are found in the emergent layer of the rainforest.

Break two or three more sticks so that they are about three-quarters the size of the first trees. Press these shorter trees, which form the rainforest's canopy layer, into the clay around the tall trees. Crumple tissue to glue around the top of the short sticks to make the leaves.

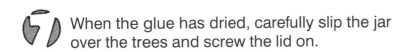 Break two or three thin twigs so that they are about half the size of the second trees. These twigs form the young trees and shrubs found in the understory of the rainforest. Cut some long, narrow leaves from green tissue paper and glue them to the tops of the twigs.

Crumple a piece of brown tissue paper and glue it over the clay around the base of the trees. This forms the carpet of moss and dead leaves that make up the forest floor.

Wrap strands of Easter grass around the tree to make vines.

When the glue has dried, carefully slip the jar over the trees and screw the lid on.

With the marker, write the name of each of the four layers of the rainforest on a strip of masking tape. Stick the labels on the jar to mark each layer.

Many animals spend their entire lives in just one layer of the rainforest.

Emergent Layer

Canopy

understory

Forest Floor

Dictyophora Fruit

Here is what you need:

cardboard tube, 5 inches (13 cm) long
two plastic six-pack ring holders
black pipe cleaner
cardboard egg carton
hole punch
scissors
white glue
paintbrush and white, green, and black poster paint
newspaper to work on

The fungus dictyophora sometimes sprouts a stem with a lacy cap with a greenish black tip that attracts flies. Spores, or seeds, stick to the flies, which spread the fungus to other parts of the rainforest.

Here is what you do:

 Paint the cardboard tube white.

 Cut two cups from the egg carton. Paint the bottoms of the two cups greenish black.

 Punch a hole in each side of one end of the cardboard tube. Punch a hole in each side of the bottom of one of the egg cups.

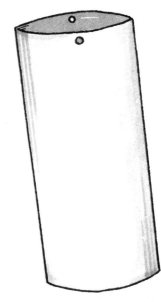

4 String a piece of pipe cleaner through the holes in the tube. Wrap the two plastic six-pack holders around the tube to form the lacy cap. Wrap the ends of the pipe cleaner around the rings to hold the rings in place. Set the egg cup with the holes on top of the tube, open end up. Insert the two ends of the pipe cleaner through the holes and twist the ends together to hold everything in place. Trim off any extra pipe cleaner that will not fit inside the cup.

5 Cut a 1/2-inch (1.3-cm) opening in the bottom of the second egg cup. Turn it over and glue the rim to the rim of the cup on the top of the tube.

If you wish, you can make one or two paper flies to glue on the top of the fungus.

Necktie Bromeliad

Here is what you need:

4 old neckties
plastic cap from fabric-softener bottle
3 rubber bands
white glue
scissors
green poster paint and paintbrush
blue tissue paper or plastic wrap
colorful construction paper scraps
markers
Styrofoam tray to work on

There are about 1,500 types of bromeliads, including Spanish moss and the pineapple plant. The leaf clusters of many bromeliads form a cup that catches rainwater.

Here is what you do:

Cut a piece off the thin end of each necktie about 3 inches (8 cm) long. These pieces will be the inner leaves of the plant. Turn the cap upside down so that it forms a cup. Arrange the four tie pieces around the cap, with the points up. Wrap a rubber band around the ties to hold them in place.

Cut seven or more pieces from the ties. Each should be about 4 inches (10 cm) long. Cut one end of each piece into a point.

3 Rub glue around the inner leaves along the sides of the cup. Stick a layer of longer tie pieces to the shorter ones, points facing outward, using a rubber band to hold them in place.

4 Cut nine or ten more pieces from the ties. Each should be about 5 inches (13 cm) long. Cut one end of each piece into a point.

5 Rub glue around the outer leaves along the sides of the cup. Stick a layer of long tie pieces to them, using another rubber band to hold them all in place.

6 Paint all of the necktie leaves green and let the plant dry on the Styrofoam tray.

7) Crumple some blue plastic wrap or tissue paper and put it inside the cup. Now you have water in the little pond.

Cut some insects out of colorful paper and draw details with the markers. Glue the insects to the leaves of the bromeliad plant.

You can also cut out some pollywogs to live in the water.

"Hand"Some Orchids

Here is what you need for each flower:

green pipe cleaner, 12 inches (30 cm) long
orange pipe cleaner, 4 inches (10 cm) long
construction paper in green and a
    bright color of your choice
pencil
scissors
cellophane tape

Here is what you do:

Trace both of your hands on the bright-colored paper. Trace one hand on the green paper. Cut out the three tracings.

Bend the orange pipe cleaner in half. Wrap one end of the green pipe cleaner around the bend, to make a stem for the flower. Bend each end of the orange pipe cleaner outward to make the stamen of the flower.

Wrap the two bright-colored hands around the stamen. Tape them in place to form the petals of the flower.

Wrap the green hand around the stamen, just below the other petals. Tape it in place to form the leaves.

There are more than 20,000 species of orchids in the world. They come in every color except black.

Make lots of flowers in all the different colors found in a rainforest.

Hercules Beetle Hat

Here is what you need:

newspaper
white glue
plastic bowl about the size you would like the hat to be
five black pipe cleaners, 12 inches (30 cm) long
hole punch
scissors
black paint and paintbrush
orange paper scrap
rubber band
ballpoint pen
extra newspaper to work on

Here is what you do:

Add a tablespoon or more of water to about 1 cup (237 ml) of glue to make the glue easier to spread. Open a double sheet of newspaper and paint one side with the watery glue. Fold the newspaper again so that the two sides are glued together. Do the same thing with another double sheet of newspaper. Glue both sheets together so that you have a stack of four sheets of newspaper.

Shape the glue-covered papers over the bottom of the plastic bowl. Hold the newspapers in place by stretching a rubber band around the rim of the bowl.

Hercules beetles are among the largest insects in the rainforest. They can grow to be 6 inches (15 cm) long.

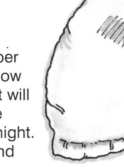 Trim off the extra newspaper below the rubber band. Now you have a bowl-shaped hat that will be the body of the beetle. Let the newspaper dry completely overnight. Then remove the rubber band and take the hat off the bowl.

Paint the beetle body black and let it dry.

Cut tiny eyes from orange paper and glue them to one side of the body.

With the hole punch, punch three holes along the rim on each side of the body. Space the holes about 1 inch (2.5 cm) apart. Cut three of the pipe cleaners in half to make six legs for the beetle. Insert the end of one pipe cleaner through each hole and wrap the end around the rim to hold the pipe cleaner in place. Bend each pipe-cleaner leg in the middle so that it curves downward.

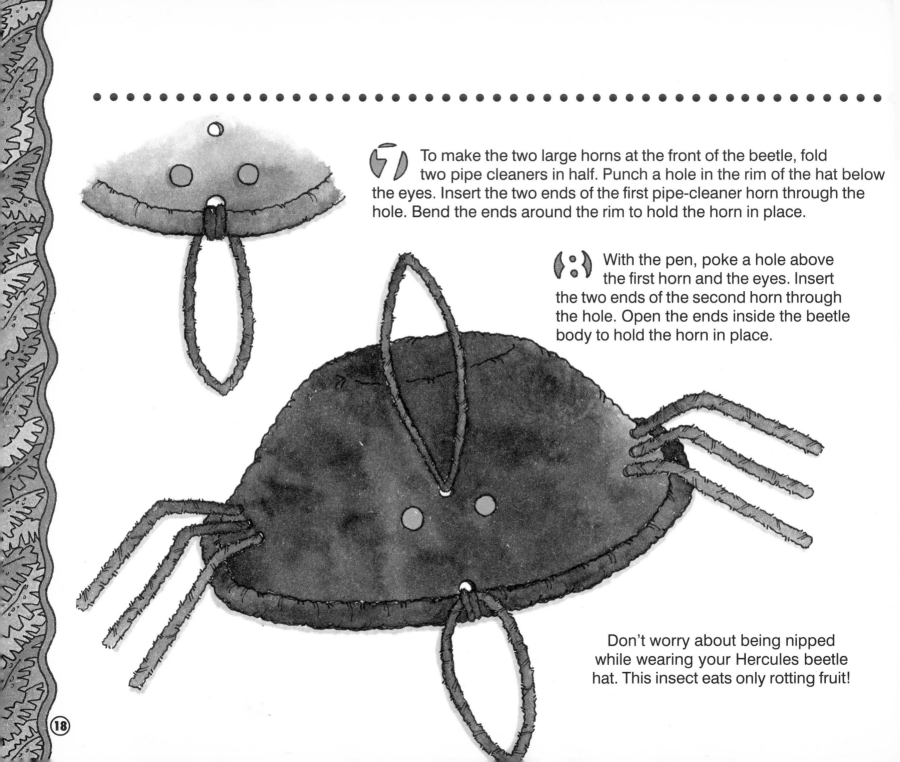

To make the two large horns at the front of the beetle, fold two pipe cleaners in half. Punch a hole in the rim of the hat below the eyes. Insert the two ends of the first pipe-cleaner horn through the hole. Bend the ends around the rim to hold the horn in place.

With the pen, poke a hole above the first horn and the eyes. Insert the two ends of the second horn through the hole. Open the ends inside the beetle body to hold the horn in place.

Don't worry about being nipped while wearing your Hercules beetle hat. This insect eats only rotting fruit!

Curly-Haired Tarantula

The curly-haired tarantula is a kind of spider. It is very strong, but does not have very good eyesight—even though it has eight eyes!

Here is what you need:

peanut with shell
black pipe cleaner, 12 inches (30 cm) long
tiny wiggle eyes, two or more
black poster paint and paintbrush
white glue
brown yarn
scissors
masking tape
Styrofoam tray to work on

Here is what you do:

1. Paint the peanut black to make the body of the spider.

2. Cut four pieces of pipe cleaner, 2 1/2 inches (6 cm) long. Twist the pieces together at their centers. Then spread all the ends open to form eight legs. Glue the legs on the bottom of the peanut. Wrap masking tape around the legs and the peanut to hold the legs in place while the glue dries.

3. Cut a piece of pipe cleaner 1 inch (2.5 cm) long. Bend it in the middle to make antennae. Glue the bend to the side of the peanut that is opposite from the legs. Glue two wiggle eyes—or more—under the antennae. Let the glue dry.

4. Cut pieces of brown yarn about 1/2 inch (1.3 cm) long. Cover the body of the spider with glue, then stick on the pieces of brown yarn. To make the spider's poisonous fangs, glue two pieces of brown yarn under the eyes of the spider.

The curly-haired tarantula is very hairy!

Tiger Centipede

Here is what you need:

two cardboard paper-towel tubes
two orange pipe cleaners, 12 inches (30 cm) long
black pipe cleaner, 12 inches (30 cm) long
orange construction paper
black and orange poster paint and paintbrush
hole punch
scissors
stapler and staples
white glue
old pair of pantyhose
black marker
newspaper to work on

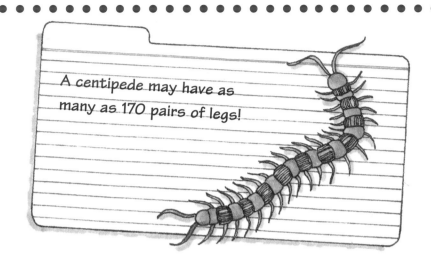

A centipede may have as many as 170 pairs of legs!

Here is what you do:

Paint one tube orange and the other black. Let the paint dry.

Cut each tube into nine equal sections.

Cut off one leg of the pantyhose.

Slip the toe of the pantyhose leg into an orange ring and staple it in place. Punch two holes opposite each other on a black ring and slip it onto the pantyhose.

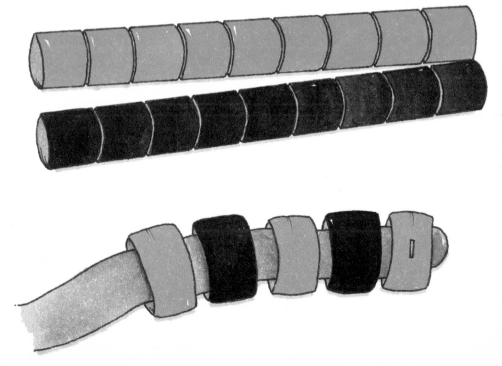

Thread alternating orange and black rings onto the pantyhose, ending with two oranges. Staple the last orange ring to what was the top of the pantyhose leg. (You will have two black rings left over.)

Cut two strips of paper, 6 inches (15 cm) wide, from the long side of the orange paper. Tape the two strips end to end. Trim the double strip to the length of the centipede, minus four rings. Fold the paper in half lengthwise and cut legs along the open end of the paper. Make one set for every segment of the body except the two front and the two rear. Open the paper up and glue the center of the paper to the centipede body so that the legs stick out on each side.

Punch two holes in the top of the single orange ring at one end of the centipede. To make the centipede's antennae, insert an orange pipe cleaner through the two holes. Twist the two ends around each other to hold the antennae in place. Spread the two ends slightly apart and bend them so that they point forward.

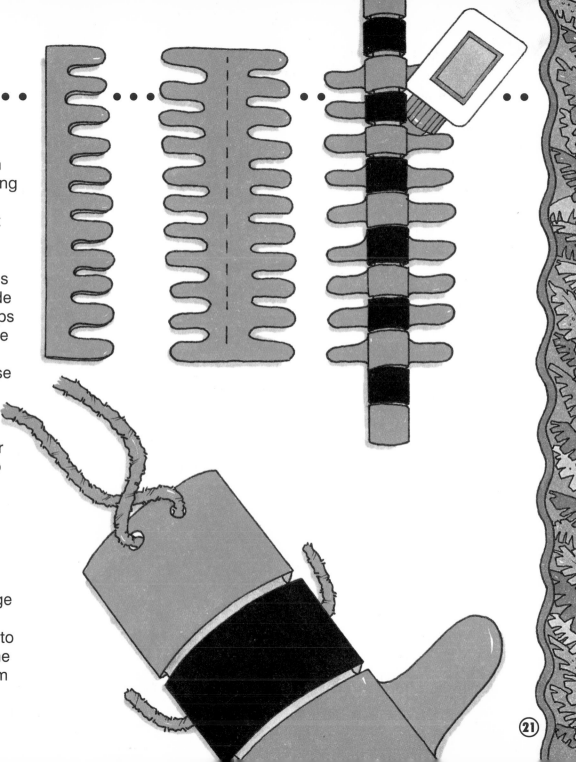

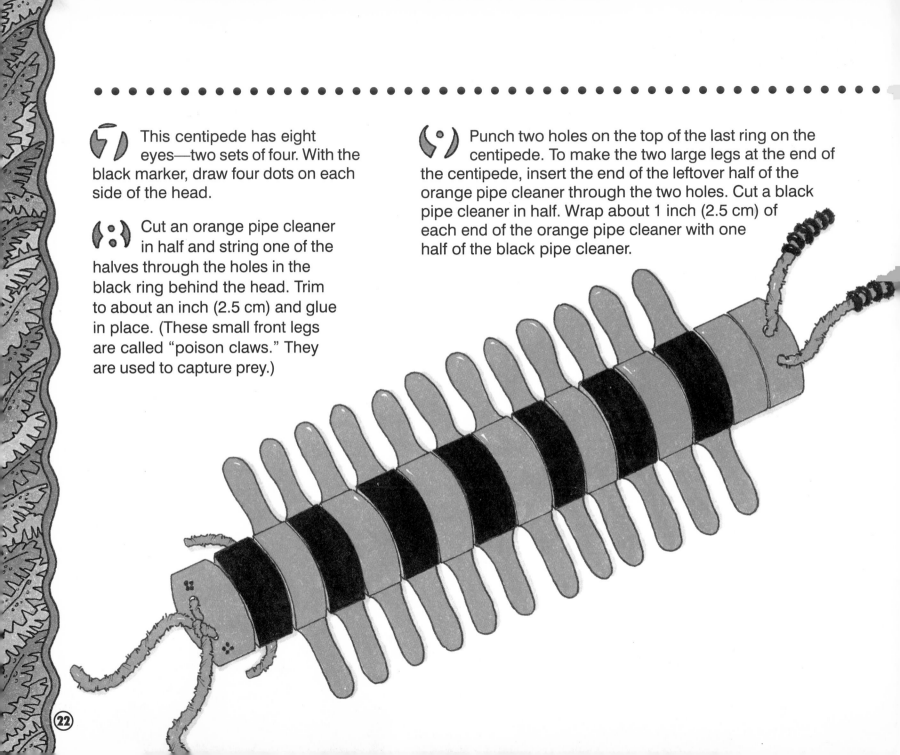

7 This centipede has eight eyes—two sets of four. With the black marker, draw four dots on each side of the head.

8 Cut an orange pipe cleaner in half and string one of the halves through the holes in the black ring behind the head. Trim to about an inch (2.5 cm) and glue in place. (These small front legs are called "poison claws." They are used to capture prey.)

9 Punch two holes on the top of the last ring on the centipede. To make the two large legs at the end of the centipede, insert the end of the leftover half of the orange pipe cleaner through the two holes. Cut a black pipe cleaner in half. Wrap about 1 inch (2.5 cm) of each end of the orange pipe cleaner with one half of the black pipe cleaner.

Emerald Tree Boa

Here is what you need:

old pair of pantyhose
Styrofoam packing pieces
black and red felt scraps
green, black, and white poster paint and paintbrush
white glue
scissors
newspaper to work on

Here is what you do:

The emerald tree boa looks like a vine—until it starts to slither.

Cut off one leg of a pair of pantyhose. Stuff the cut-off leg with Styrofoam packing pieces to the snake's body. Knot the end of the stocking to it. Trim off the extra stocking around the knot.

Paint the snake's body green. Dab the top of the snake with black and white paint to make a shadowy pattern.

Cut two pieces of black felt to make slanted snake eyes. Glue the eyes on the top of the snake body at the toe end of the stocking.

Cut a long red forked tongue from the red felt. Glue the tongue under the head of the snake.

Find a nice tree for your emerald boa to hang out in.

Common Iguana

Here is what you need:

two cardboard toilet-tissue tubes
one cardboard paper-towel tube
cereal-box cardboard
green tissue paper
orange construction paper
black marker
masking tape
green and orange poster paint and paintbrush
scissors
newspaper to work on

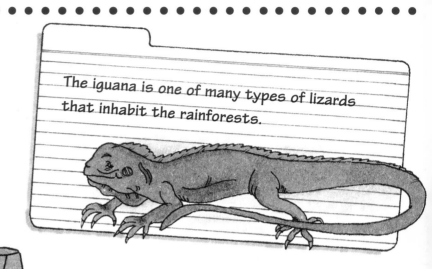

The iguana is one of many types of lizards that inhabit the rainforests.

Here is what you do:

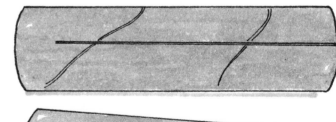 Cut a slit 3 inches (8 cm) long in the toilet-tissue tubes. Overlap the cut edges to form a cone shape. Use masking tape to hold the edges in place. This will be the head of the iguana.

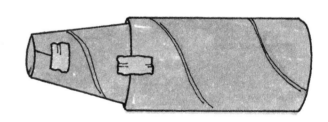 Cut a slit in the other side of the head. Overlap the cut edges just enough so that the end of the cone fits inside one end of the other toilet-tissue tube. Tape the two tubes together. They form the head and body of the iguana.

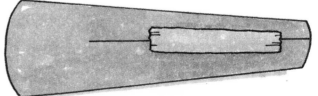 Cut a slit in the paper-towel tube, leaving 1 inch (2.5 cm) uncut at one end. Overlap the edges of the tube to form a long cone shape. This is the iguana's tail. Tape the cone shape to hold it in place.

4 Cut a small slit in the other end of the tail tube. Overlap the edges just enough so that the end of the cone fits inside the open end of the body. Tape the tail to the body.

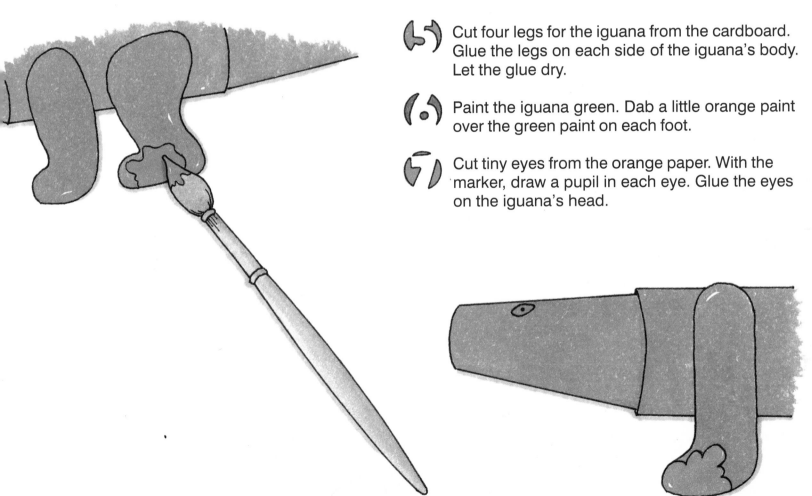

5 Cut four legs for the iguana from the cardboard. Glue the legs on each side of the iguana's body. Let the glue dry.

6 Paint the iguana green. Dab a little orange paint over the green paint on each foot.

7 Cut tiny eyes from the orange paper. With the marker, draw a pupil in each eye. Glue the eyes on the iguana's head.

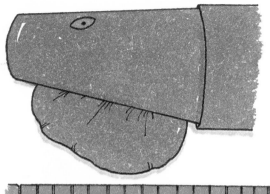

Cut a piece of green tissue paper, 2 inches (5 cm) by 3 inches (8 cm). Round off the edges of the paper. An iguana has skin that hangs down under its chin. Gather one side of the paper slightly. Glue the gathered side under the iguana's chin.

Cut a strip of paper 2 inches (5 cm) wide and as long as the iguana, from its head to its tail. Cut fringe along the length of one edge of the paper. Glue the other edge of the paper to the iguana, so that the fringe sticks up. Trim the fringe so that it is longest at the head and shortest at the tail.

Make some rainforest insects for
your iguana to eat.

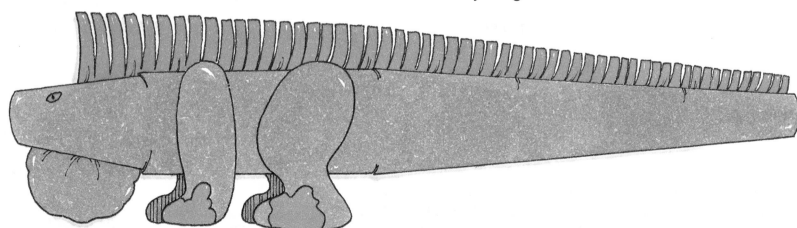

Necktie Snake

Here is what you need:

old colorful necktie
three pipe cleaners, 12 inches (30 cm) long
red felt
scissors
white glue
tiny craft jewels (or black felt)
clamp clothespin

The colorful snakes that fill the rainforest can grow to giant size.

Here is what you do:

Cut the necktie in half crosswise. The thin half will be the snake's body.

Insert the pipe cleaners in the thin half of the tie.

Cut a long forked tongue from red felt. Glue the tongue under the point of the tie.

Fold the other, open end of the snake body into a triangle point and glue it shut. Use a clamp clothespin to hold the folds in place until the glue dries.

Glue two tiny jewel eyes to the top of the snake's head to give the snake a mysterious look. (You can make the eyes out of felt if you do not have jewels.)

Bend the pipe cleaners inside the snake to position it with its head up, ready to strike its prey.

Tree Frog Beanbag

Here is what you need:

old red adult-size sock
dark-blue felt
two white 1-inch (2.5-cm) pom-poms
dried beans
plastic sandwich bag
hole punch
scissors
white glue
clamp clothespin

Many kinds of brightly colored frogs live in the rainforest. You might want to use a different color for each frog you make.

Here is what you do:

Cut a piece off the foot of the sock, about 5 inches (13 cm) from the toe. The cut piece will be the body of the frog.

Pour enough dried beans into the sock to fill it about three-quarters full. Dump the beans into the plastic bag. Fold over the open end of the bag and put the bag in the sock.

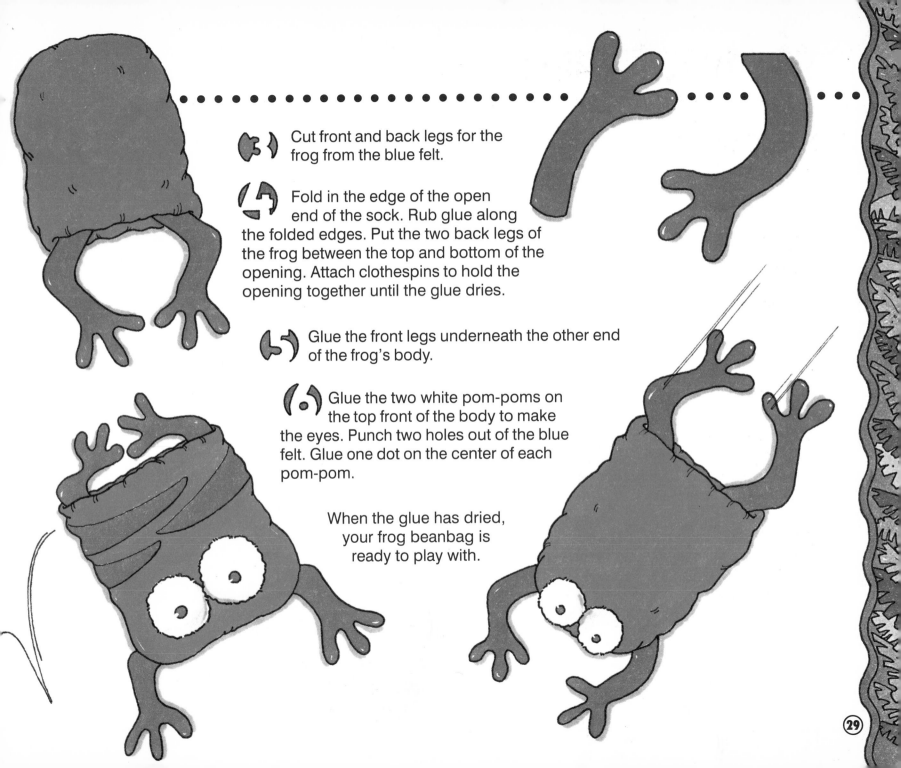

3) Cut front and back legs for the frog from the blue felt.

4) Fold in the edge of the open end of the sock. Rub glue along the folded edges. Put the two back legs of the frog between the top and bottom of the opening. Attach clothespins to hold the opening together until the glue dries.

5) Glue the front legs underneath the other end of the frog's body.

6) Glue the two white pom-poms on the top front of the body to make the eyes. Punch two holes out of the blue felt. Glue one dot on the center of each pom-pom.

When the glue has dried, your frog beanbag is ready to play with.

Hummingbird and Flower Puppets

Here is what you need:

old knit adult-size glove
flexi-straw
craft feathers
two tiny wiggle eyes
pink felt
yellow, blue, and green poster paint and paintbrush
white glue
scissors

Here is what you do:

Cut off two fingers of the knit glove to use for the puppets.

Paint the tip of one glove finger yellow to make the center of the flower finger puppet. Cut a flower shape about 5 inches (13 cm) wide from the pink felt. Cut a slit 1 inch (2.5 cm) wide in the center of the flower and slip the flower over the painted tip of the finger. Cut a second flower shape about 4 inches (10 cm) wide. Cut a slit 1 inch (2.5 cm) wide in the center of that flower. Slip the second flower on top of the first one to complete your flower finger puppet.

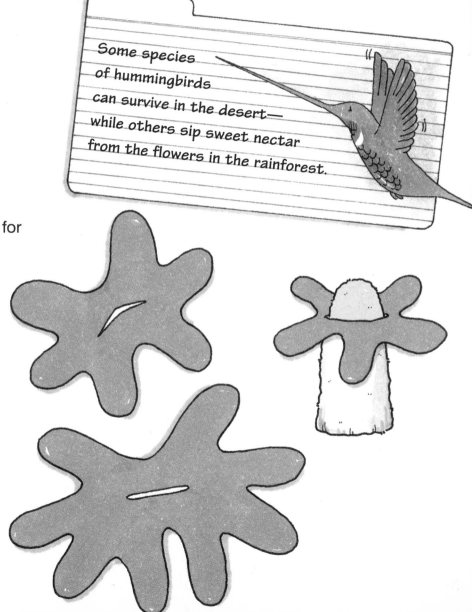

Some species of hummingbirds can survive in the desert—while others sip sweet nectar from the flowers in the rainforest.

3) To make the hummingbird puppet, paint the other glove finger with blue and green paint.

4) Cut a tiny slit in the tip of the glove finger. Slide the top end of the flexi-straw into the bottom of the glove finger and out the tiny slit. Bend the straw to form the long beak of the hummingbird. The other end of the straw is a holder for the puppet.

5) Glue two tiny wiggle eyes to the head of the bird. Glue on colorful craft feathers to make the outspread wings and the tail of the bird.

Put the flower puppet on the finger of one of your hands. With the other hand, fly the hummingbird over for a sip of nectar.

Window Toucan

Here is what you need:

small sheet of light-green construction paper
black and light-blue construction paper
yellow, green, orange, and red tissue paper
red yarn
hole punch
scissors
white glue
pencil

Here is what you do:

Although the toucan has become a symbol of the rainforest, there are 131 species, many of which live in other habitats.

Turn the light-green paper so that its longest edges are at the top and bottom. With the pencil, sketch a large toucan beak on the paper. Cut out the beak shape, without cutting through any of the sides of the paper.

Cut a half circle out of the black paper to make the head of the toucan. Glue the straight edge of the half circle to the edge of the green paper. The curved side of the half circle should slightly overlap the widest part of the beak.

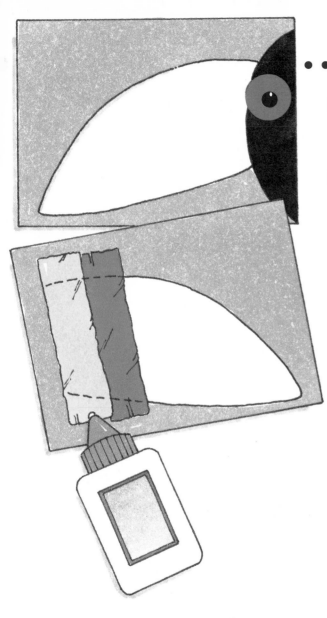

3) Cut an eye from the blue paper and a pupil from the black paper. Glue the pupil in the center of the eye. Glue the eye on the head of the toucan.

4) Cut strips of colorful tissue. Glue the strips across the back of the paper to fill in the opening you made when you cut out the toucan's beak. Cut as many tissue-paper strips as you need to fill the entire opening.

5) Punch a hole close to each side of the top of the paper. Cut a long piece of yarn. Thread the yarn through the two holes and tie the ends together to make a hanger for the toucan.

Hang the toucan in a sunny window so that the light can shine through the colorful beak.

Foot and Hands Macaw

Here is what you need:

construction paper in several bright colors
black construction paper scrap
pencil
scissors

Here is what you do:

Trace around your shoe on a piece of brightly colored paper. Cut the shoe shape out to use for the body of the bird, with the heel end forming the head.

Cut two black eyes and glue them to the head. Cut a curved beak from yellow paper and glue it below the bird's eyes. Cut out two claw feet from the black paper. Glue the feet to the bottom of the bird.

Macaws are very beautiful parrots, but they are not often kept as pets as they tend to scream rather than talk—and they may bite!

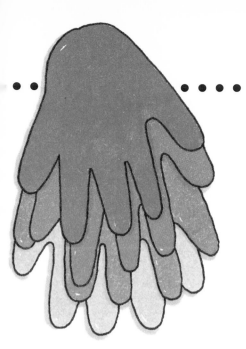

Trace around your hand on a different color of paper than you used for the body of the bird. Stack the paper on three other colors of paper and cut the hand shape out. Glue the four hand shapes together in a row with the fingers of each hand hanging down below the fingers of the hand above it to form a tail. Glue the tail to the back bottom of the bird so that the fingers hang down to look like tail feathers.

Stack two pieces of each of three different colors of paper. Trace your hand on the top piece of paper. Cut the hand shape out. Glue three different color hand shapes together in the same way you glued the tail, to make each of the bird's wings. Glue one wing on the bird sticking out from behind the left side. Glue the other wing to the front of the bird and sticking out from the right side.

You can be creative with the colors you use for your bird or you can copy one of the color combinations of a real macaw. You can find pictures of different macaws at the library.

Fruit Bat

Here is what you need:

old adult-size brown sock
brown construction paper
black marker
scissors
white glue
wire hanger
5 black pipe cleaners, each 12 inches (30 cm) long
fiberfill
old pantyhose
three large safety pins
masking tape

Fruit-eating bats spread seeds throughout rainforests, thus helping the plants to regenerate.

Here is what you do:

Cut off the cuff of the sock. To make the bat's body, stuff the foot of the sock with fiberfill. Close the sock by wrapping half a pipe cleaner tightly around the opening. Bend the two ends of the pipe cleaner to make the bat's legs. Cut two pieces of pipe cleaner 1 inch (2.5 cm) long. Wrap one short piece of pipe cleaner around each leg, about 3/4 inch (2 cm) from the end. Bend all the pipe-cleaner ends to make toes for the bat.

Cut ears, eyes, and nose holes from the brown paper. With the marker, add pupils to the eyes. Glue the features to the front of the bat to make its face.

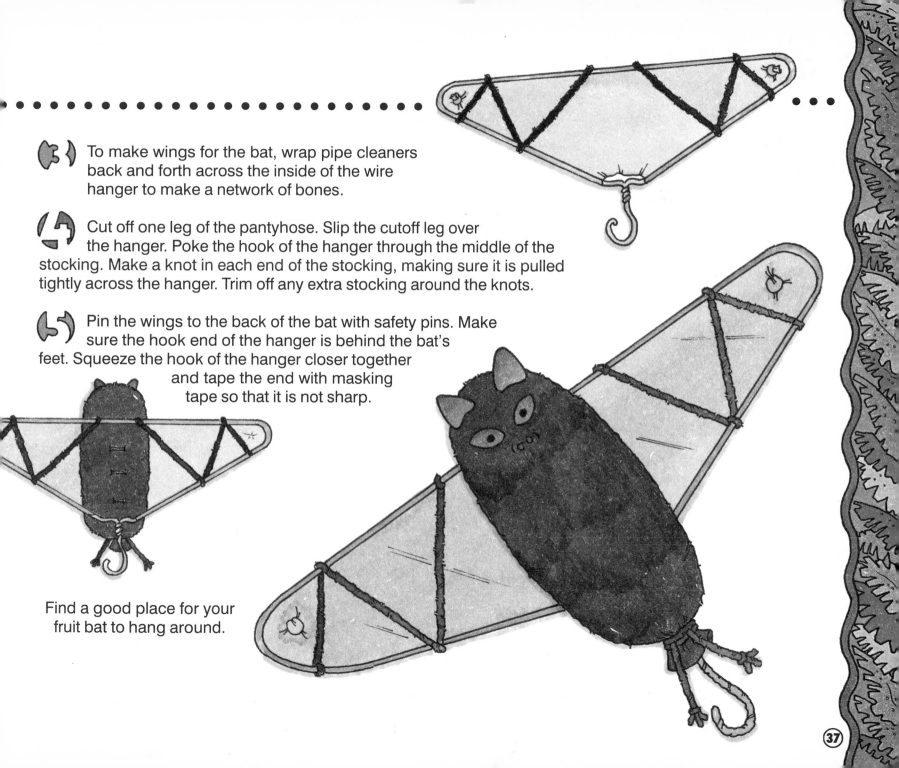

3 To make wings for the bat, wrap pipe cleaners back and forth across the inside of the wire hanger to make a network of bones.

4 Cut off one leg of the pantyhose. Slip the cutoff leg over the hanger. Poke the hook of the hanger through the middle of the stocking. Make a knot in each end of the stocking, making sure it is pulled tightly across the hanger. Trim off any extra stocking around the knots.

5 Pin the wings to the back of the bat with safety pins. Make sure the hook end of the hanger is behind the bat's feet. Squeeze the hook of the hanger closer together and tape the end with masking tape so that it is not sharp.

Find a good place for your fruit bat to hang around.

Harpy Eagle Body Puppet

Here is what you need:

two large brown grocery bags
orange and brown construction paper
black marker
brown yarn
brown craft feathers
white fiberfill
scissors
white glue
hole reinforcers
hole punch
two large rubber bands

Here is what you do:

The magnificent harpy eagle—one of the largest birds in the rainforest—is a rare sight to see. There are very few harpy eagles left. This bird does not soar through the skies. Instead, it dives swiftly from its roost to catch its prey.

Close one bag so that the bottom folds over onto one side. The bottom of the bag will be the head of the eagle, and the bag will be the body. Cover the head and body with glue. Stick pieces of fiberfill on the glue to make the eagle's white feathers.

Cut two eyes from the brown paper. Add pupils with a marker. Glue the eyes on the head. Cut a beak from orange paper. Glue the beak under the flap of the head. To make the eagle's double crest, glue a craft feather above each eye.

3) Punch a hole on each side of the bag behind the head. Cover each hole with a reinforcer. Cut a piece of yarn about 4 feet (120 cm) long. String the ends of the yarn through both holes. Tie the two ends together, leaving the yarn just long enough so that when you slip the yarn around your neck, the bird hangs down in front of you—just below your chin. Trim off any extra yarn.

4) Cut open the seam of the second brown bag. Cut the bottom out so that you have a flat piece of brown paper. Cut two large wings for the eagle about 12 inches (30 cm) wide and 18 inches (46 cm) long. Glue one wing in the fold on each side of the bag, just below the eagle's head.

5) Punch a hole in the top end of each wing, about 3 inches (8 cm) from the tip. Stick a hole reinforcer on the back of each hole. Thread a rubber band through each hole, then loop one end of the rubber band through the other end. When you slip your hands through the rubber-band holders, you can open the wings of the body puppet.

Cut two tail feathers from the brown-bag scraps, about 12 inches (30 cm) long and 6 inches (15 cm) wide. Glue the tops of the tail feathers to the inside of the back of the bag. The harpy eagle's tail feathers have brown and white stripes. Glue strips of white fiberfill across the front of the tail feathers to make stripes.

Cut two feet, each with three claws, from the orange paper. With the black marker, color in the claws at the end of each foot. Glue the top of the claws to the inside of the front of the bag so that they hang down in front of the tail feathers.

To use your harpy eagle body puppet, slip the yarn around your neck and put a rubber-band holder around each wrist.

Spotted Cats

Here is what you need:

orange, white, and light-green construction paper
black and orange paint and paintbrush
markers
white glue
scissors

Here is what you do:

Large spotted cats like the jaguar, leopard, and ocelot live in the rainforests. The different sizes and fur patterns can help you to identify each type of cat.

For each cat you wish to make, paint your hand orange and make a handprint on the white construction paper. Cut out all the handprints.

For each hand body, cut out a cat's head from the orange paper. With markers, draw a face on each head. Turn your handprints upside down and glue a head to the palm, opposite the thumb. The thumb forms the tail of the cat, and the fingers form the legs.

Dip your finger in black paint and give each cat lots of spots.

With the markers, draw a rainforest environment for the cats on the light-green construction paper. Glue the cats on the rainforest picture.

Find pictures of different species of big cats and fill your rainforest with them.

Anteater Puppet

Here is what you need:

brown or gray paper
pencil
stapler and staples
scissors
red pipe cleaner, 12 inches (30 cm) long
plastic straw
Velcro sticky dot
black felt scraps
black marker

Tamandua anteaters live in the trees of the rainforest and eat ants with their very long tongues.

Here is what you do:

Fold a large sheet of brown paper in half. Draw a pencil sketch of an anteater on the paper. Cut out the anteater, cutting through both pieces of paper.

Staple the two sides of the anteater together at the top and the bottom of the head and body. Leave the back open so you can fit your hand in to work the puppet.

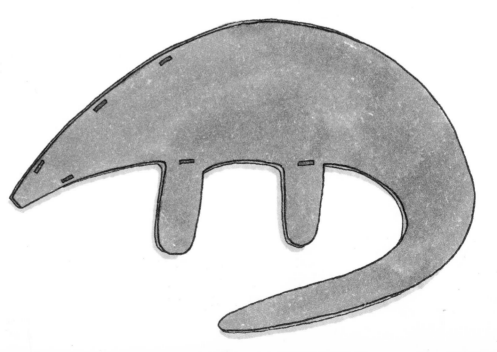

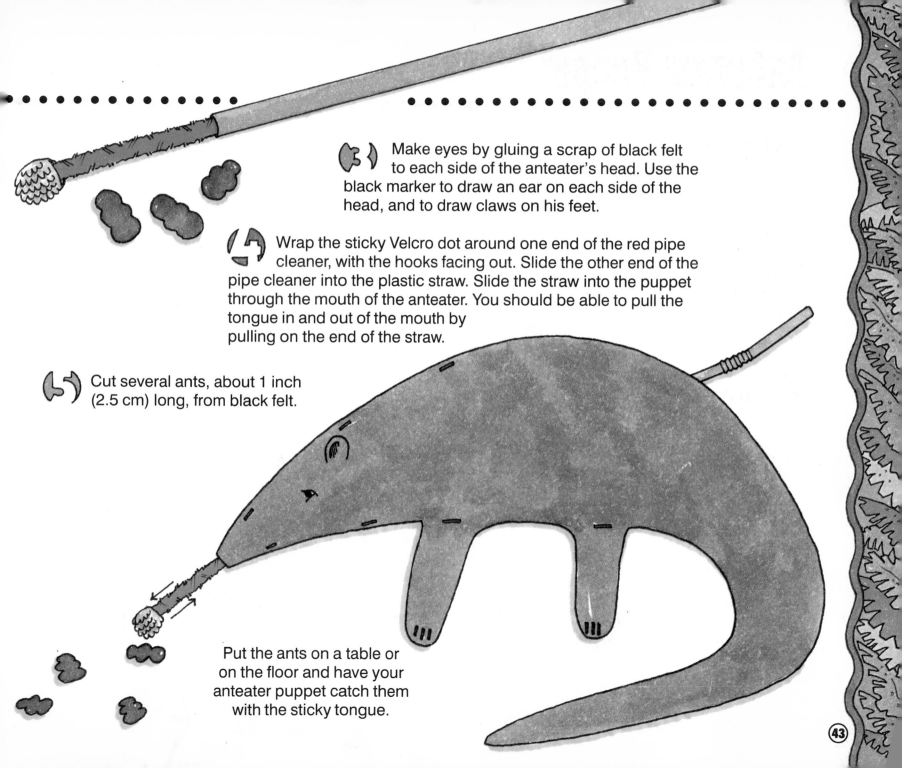

Make eyes by gluing a scrap of black felt to each side of the anteater's head. Use the black marker to draw an ear on each side of the head, and to draw claws on his feet.

Wrap the sticky Velcro dot around one end of the red pipe cleaner, with the hooks facing out. Slide the other end of the pipe cleaner into the plastic straw. Slide the straw into the puppet through the mouth of the anteater. You should be able to pull the tongue in and out of the mouth by pulling on the end of the straw.

Cut several ants, about 1 inch (2.5 cm) long, from black felt.

Put the ants on a table or on the floor and have your anteater puppet catch them with the sticky tongue.

Howling Howler Monkey Mask

Here is what you need:

cardboard paper-towel tube
paper plate, 9 inches (23 cm) in diameter
two paper plates, 7 inches (18 cm) in diameter
black, brown, and white construction-paper scraps
reddish brown yarn
black poster paint and paintbrush
white glue
scissors
newspaper to work on

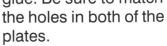

The call of the howler monkey can be heard up to a mile and a half (2.5 km) away.

Here is what you do:

Cut six slits 1 1/2 inches (4 cm) long around one end of the cardboard tube. Bend all the cut pieces away from the tube.

Near the edge of the large plate, trace around the uncut end of the tube. Cut out the traced circle.

Trace another circle in the middle of the bottom half of one of the small plates. Cut out the circle. Stack the two small plates together and use the hole in the first plate to trace a circle on the second small plate. Cut that circle out, too.

Push the uncut end of the tube through the hole in one of the small plates, from the underside of the plate to the top. Push the tube through until the cut pieces rest on the bottom of the plate. Rub glue all over the bottom of the plate and the cut ends of the tube. Press the other small plate on top of the glue. Be sure to match the holes in both of the plates.

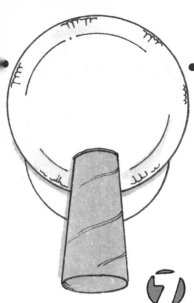

 Slide the large plate over the tube, so that the bottom of the large plate rests on the two small plates. The large plate forms the monkey's head, and the smaller plates form the monkey's muzzle. Glue the larger plate to the smaller plates.

6 Paint the front of the monkey's face black.

7 Cut eyes, ears, and a nose from the construction-paper scraps and glue them in place.

8 To make fur, cut lots of snips of yarn, about 1 inch (2.5 cm) long. Glue them all over the head of the monkey and around the muzzle.

Howl and bark through the tube, just like a noisy howler monkey.

Spider Monkey Mobile

Here is what you need:

large tree branch
green tissue paper, in one or more shades
brown, black, and light-brown construction paper
black or brown pipe cleaners, each 12 inches (30 cm) long
hole punch
scissors
stapler and staples
white glue
yarn

Spider monkeys swing through the trees of the rainforests using their arms, legs, and tails.

Here is what you do:

1 Cut a long piece of yarn to tie to each end of the branch to make a hanger for the mobile.

2 Cut green tissue paper into 2-inch (5-cm) squares. Crumple the center of each square and glue the squares to the branch to make leaves. Cover the branch with tissue leaves.

3 To make each adult monkey, cut two identical oval shapes, about 4 inches (10 cm) tall, from brown paper. Cut five pieces of pipe cleaner, each 4 inches (10 cm) long, for each monkey's tail, arms, and legs.

Staple the two ovals together with the pipe cleaners placed between the layers. Place a staple over each arm and leg and over the tail.

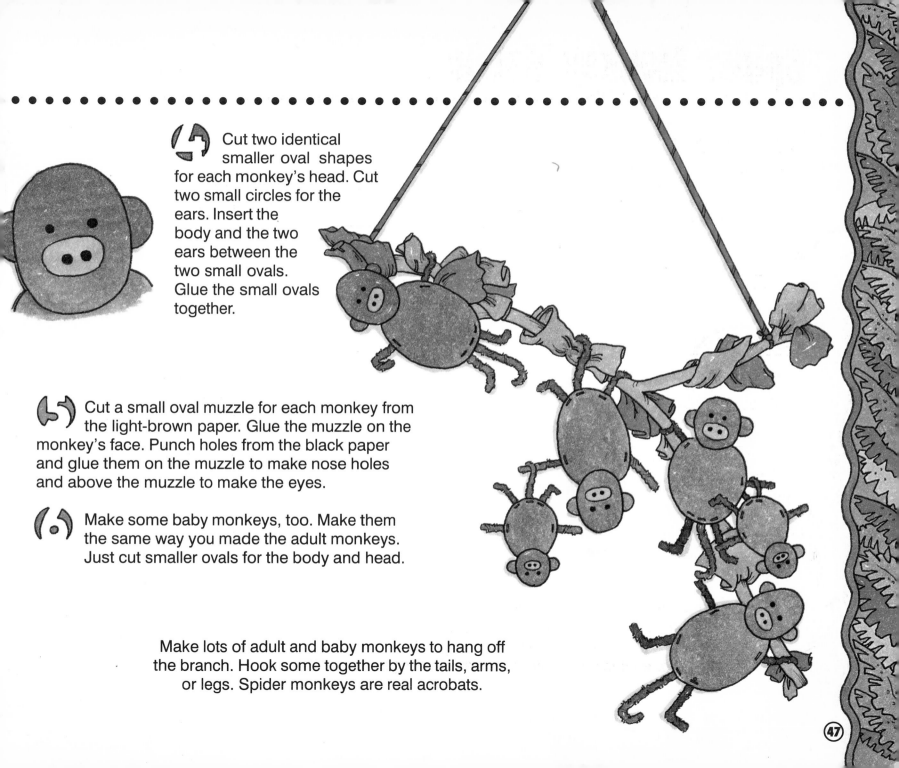

Cut two identical smaller oval shapes for each monkey's head. Cut two small circles for the ears. Insert the body and the two ears between the two small ovals. Glue the small ovals together.

Cut a small oval muzzle for each monkey from the light-brown paper. Glue the muzzle on the monkey's face. Punch holes from the black paper and glue them on the muzzle to make nose holes and above the muzzle to make the eyes.

Make some baby monkeys, too. Make them the same way you made the adult monkeys. Just cut smaller ovals for the body and head.

Make lots of adult and baby monkeys to hang off the branch. Hook some together by the tails, arms, or legs. Spider monkeys are real acrobats.

Books About Rainforests

Cherry, Lynne. *The Great Kapok Tree*. Orlando, FL: Harcourt Brace & Co., 1990.

Cowcher, Helen. *Rain Forest.* New York: Farrar, Straus, & Giroux, Inc., 1988.

Darling, Kathy. *Rain Forest Babies.* New York: Walker Publishing, 1996.

Dunphy, Madeline. *Here Is the Tropical Rainforest.* New York: Hyperion Books for Children, 1994.

Gibbons, Gail. *Nature's Green Umbrella: Tropical Rain Forests.* New York: Morrow Junior Books, 1994.

Jeunese, Gillimand and Mettler, Rene. *The Rain Forest.* New York: Scholastic, Inc., 1994.

Jordan, Martin and Tanis. *Journey of the Red-Eyed Tree Frog.* New York: Green Tiger Press, 1992.

Lepthien, Emilie. *Tropical Rainforests.* Danbury, CT: Childrens Press, 1993.

Lessen, Don. *Inside the Amazing Amazon.* New York: Crown Publishing Group, 1995.

Patent, Dorothy Hinshaw. *Children Save the Rainforest.* New York: Cobble Hill Books, 1996.

Ricciuti, Edward. *Rainforest.* Tarrytown, NY: Marshall Cavendish, 1994.

Ryder, Joanne and Rothman, Michael. *Jaguar in the Rain Forest.* New York: Morrow Junior Books, 1996.

Sayre, April. *Tropical Rainforest.* New York: Twenty-First Century Books, 1994.

Sirace, Carolyn. *Rainforest.* Austin, TX: Steck-Vaughn, 1994.

Warburton, Lois. *Rain Forest.* San Diego, CA: Lucent Books, Inc., 1991.

Willow, Diane. *At Home in the Rainforest.* Watertown, MA: Charlesbridge Publishing, 1991.

Yolen, Jane. *Welcome to the Greenhouse*. New York: Scholastic, Inc., 1994.